D1165063

Why People Get Tattoos and Other Body Art

31221000759741

Jeanne Nagle

ROSEN
PUBLISHING®
New York

To Emily. She has her reasons.

Published in 2012 by The Rosen Publishing Group, Inc.
29 East 21st Street, New York, NY 10010

Library of Congress Cataloging-in-Publication Data

Nagle, Jeanne.
Why people get tattoos and other body art / Jeanne Nagle.—1st ed.
    p. cm.—(Tattooing)
Includes bibliographical references and index.
ISBN 978-1-4488-4617-7 (library binding)
ISBN 978-1-4488-4620-7 (pbk.)
ISBN 978-1-4488-4741-9 (6-pack)
1. Tattooing—Juvenile literature. 2. Body marking—Juvenile literature.
I. Title.
GN419.3.N34 2012
391.6'5—dc22

2011000276

Manufactured in Malaysia

CPSIA Compliance Information: Batch #S11YA: For further information, contact Rosen Publishing, New York, New York, at 1-800-237-9932.

On the cover: Top: Mehndi, a traditional form of Indian body art. Bottom: A member of the U.S. Marine Corps (USMC) proudly wears an identifying tattoo across his upper back.

Contents

INTRODUCTION

People seem to like tinkering with their image. Trying a new hairstyle or color, buying the latest fashions, applying makeup in a unique way—these are all examples of fairly simple changes that can be made to an individual's look. There are some modifications that are more permanent than a simple change of clothes, however. Cosmetic changes made to the body for spiritual, fashion, social, or personal reasons are known as body modifications. This umbrella term includes piercing, tattooing, earlobe stretching, branding, and scarification, as well as surgical choices such as dental, facial, or breast implants.

There is a difference between modifications done for cosmetic reasons—to artfully change one's body—and medically necessary procedures. For instance, someone who has lost teeth in an accident might have dental implants in order to bite and chew food properly. Someone who has veneers, or false fronts, placed on their teeth to make a prettier, whiter smile generally does so for nonmedical reasons. They are simply modifying their appearance. Likewise, implants given to cancer patients who have had one or both breasts removed are done as a result of a medical procedure, as opposed to surgical implants for cosmetic reasons.

Tattoos and piercings are among the forms of body modification also known as adornment. These particular adornments are more popular than ever before, especially in the United States. It is a trend that started spiking in the 1990s and has grown steadily since. Tattooing has become especially trendy among young people.

There are differences between tattooing and other types of body modifications. The main difference is that while hair color will grow out, tattooing is considered permanent. So are piercings, since even if the hole heals, some type of scar or mark usually remains. The decision to permanently alter one's body is a serious one. A person should never get a tattoo or piercing as a way to fit in or try out a passing style or trend. The first step in making a wise decision about whether or not to get a modification is to be well informed about the benefits and risks associated with it.

The decision to get a tattoo or piercing itself is a very personal matter. There are as many reasons to get a tattoo, piercing, or other type of body modification as there are people who choose to have these procedures done. Yet there are a handful of reasons that seem to be pretty common. The top five of those are discussed in these pages.

CHAPTER 1

Self-Expression and Self-Image

There are a number of ways people can express their individuality, which is the combination of thoughts, feelings, and beliefs that make them unique. Writing, music, and art are a few of the more common forms of self-expression. Hobbies also reveal a bit about an individual's personality and interests. Another way people can leave their mark is through their appearance. People can control the image they present to the world through the way they dress, how they style their hair, whether or not they wear makeup, and other cosmetic modifications to their looks.

Because tattoos and piercings help them change their appearance, many people, particularly those in their teens and twenties, believe tattoos and piercings are an excellent form of self-expression. According to a 2006 study conducted by the Pew Research Center, an estimated 36 percent of Americans ages eighteen to twenty-five have at least one tattoo. Of course, if so many people are inking

A tattoo artist fills in the color of an extensive tattoo that has been outlined on a client's back and arms.

and piercing their skin, it might be hard to see how taking part in such practices is a way to express individuality. The secret is that getting a tattooed image or piercing is a very personal matter and therefore unique. Many others may choose the exact same tattoo image or piercing jewelry, but these items will look different on, and mean different things to, each wearer.

Sean's Story

Sean was fifteen when he got his ear pierced. He followed that up with a pierced nipple at sixteen and a tattoo on his shoulder a week after turning eighteen. "I just wanted to look cool," he says of these body adornments. But truth be told, there's a little more to the story than that.

"The piercings have always been a social signal that I was not the little boy that I looked like," he admits. "I felt it necessary to share my 'dark side' with everyone. The first tattoo is nothing more than a symbol of eighteen-year-old stupidity, but I sometimes pass it off as a totem of power. Plus it kinda makes my shoulder look awesome."

As he got older, Sean got another tattoo and several additional piercings, including his eyebrow and tongue. He had to cover his tattoos and take the jewelry out of his visible piercings while at work. The hassle caused him to lose interest in piercings for several years. Then he saw a graduate school classmate with unusual piercings on her collarbone. After seeing that, Sean's fascination with the procedure was back with a vengeance. "Now, I think about piercings all the time," he says.

Now twenty-nine and a new father, he thinks his tattoos and piercings will act as an icebreaker when it comes time to discuss body modification and other important topics with his children in the future.

Mementos and Remembrance

There are times in people's lives when they may discover a new passion in their life, or they merely take part in an activity that makes them happy and has a positive influence on them. It is only natural that they would want to keep that excitement and happiness alive. In this case, a tattoo becomes a lasting reminder of how they feel at that moment.

Getting inked as part of a journey may have its roots in sailors of long ago voyaging to the Polynesian islands, where they first saw tattooed flesh on the natives. Regardless of when or why it happened, the practice of getting a tattoo as a souvenir is pretty common. Tattoos of landmarks, such as the Eiffel Tower or the Empire State Building, may be chosen as a visual reminder of a favorite trip. At other times, a simple design might do the trick. For instance, the number of Peace Corps volunteers in

This traditional Samoan band design tattoo has the name of the country added as a special touch.

Samoa who get traditional tribal tattoos, mainly arm or leg bands with geometric patterns and shapes, as a memento of their time on the island is quite high and rising.

Others get a tattoo to remain close to someone or something they may have lost. Many people get tattoos that are connected to a friend or family member who has died. Getting a tattoo of this kind keeps the person who is gone permanently close. Honoring a loved one can be as simple as having a tattoo artist ink the person's initials or as complex as getting an image of the person copied from a photograph.

Life-Changing Events

The decision to get such a permanent and drastic form of modification also may be influenced by what's going on in someone's life. Significant events and experiences, whether they are considered good or bad, can make someone feel like a new or different person. That can lead to the decision to look different as well, as a reflection of these feelings.

Major events that might make someone feel like a new person—one who desires a different look with tattoos or piercings—include turning a milestone age (like twenty-one), getting married, having a baby, or surviving a medical crisis.

Medical and Paramedical Tattooing

There are several connections between medicine and tattooing. Certain medical procedures rely on tattoos so that patients can be treated effectively and safely. For instance, cancer patients undergoing radiation treatment are tattooed with small marks that allow doctors to target the area that is supposed to receive radiation. That way the surrounding,

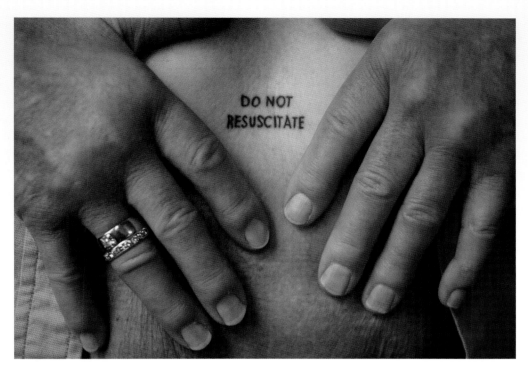

Sometimes a tattoo can alert medical personnel to a problem or a patient's wishes if he or she is unable to speak.

healthy tissue does not get zapped accidentally. Because the tattoos are permanent, there is no danger of them disappearing or shifting position.

A 2009 report by the American Association of Clinical Endocrinologists stated that more patients are choosing to have medical alerts tattooed onto their skin. This is an increasingly popular trend with those who have chronic diseases such as diabetes. Medical alert tattoos are an alternative to bracelets or necklaces that let health care providers know about a medical condition if patients are unconscious or otherwise unable to communicate with the doctor.

There are also post-treatment medical applications of tattoos. Some people go through an illness and medical treatments that may disfigure them, spoiling their appearance in some way. These individuals might turn to tattooing to hide scars or simply make them feel attractive and whole again. Tattoo artists can lessen and beautify the appearance of scars by incorporating them into their designs, lessening and beautifying their appearance. For example, cancer patients who have lost their hair might opt to get permanent eyebrow or eyelash tattoos.

Another way to hide scars is through a tattooing process called micropigmentation. Matching pigment (the color part of ink) to a patient's skin tone, a tattoo artist who specializes in this type of work can inject color underneath the top layer of skin. The result is that white marks from scarring become flesh colored.

Pride

Getting a tattoo or piercing is usually a sign that someone takes pride in his or her appearance. After all, people who don't care what they look like wouldn't bother decorating their body with permanent designs and jewelry. But there is another type of pride associated with tattooing, and that is pride in one's identity.

A shamrock is universally recognized as an Irish symbol. People who are proud of their Irish heritage may get a shamrock tattoo.

Elements of a person's identity that he or she might want to boast about through a tattoo include nationality, family heritage, and career and personal accomplishments. For example, people who are proud of being from a certain country might have that nation's flag inked onto their skin. Members of a proud Irish family might get a shamrock or a claddagh (heart with two hands and a crown) tattoo.

Inspiration

Tattoos can also serve as a symbol of inspiration. There are designs that can give their wearer the courage to take action or go forward with a plan. Sometimes the meaning is clear. Runners might get wings inked onto their ankle or foot, as a symbol of the speed they hope to have during races. Then there are quotes and phrases that offer motivation. Chinese characters are a tremendously popular type of tattoo. The marks are meant to symbolize words such as "strength" and "peace." At other times a tattoo or piercing will not convey any special meaning. It may just be meant to be colorful and attractive, which inspires wearers to be happy with their appearance.

CHAPTER 2

Culture

Body modification can be a form of self-expression. In the bigger picture, however, it can also be considered a type of cultural expression. A group of people who share similar attitudes, values, beliefs, and traditions is known as a culture. The traditions that people in a culture share may involve tattooing and piercing.

Tattooing Around the World

Tattooing has a long, involved past in many Polynesian cultures. Natives of Samoa have the *tatu*, which is where the English word "tattoo" originated. The Maori call the practice of skin marking *moko*, while the early Hawaiians called it *kakau*. All of these tattooing traditions are performed in much the same way, but each culture—and even certain groups within a culture—has its own designs.

There were a number of reasons behind each culture's practice of body art. One of the main reasons was to help show where a person stood in his or her community. Class roles

For centuries, Maori men have gotten intricate tattoos all over their bodies, including their faces. Certain designs indicate a person's place in Maori society.

were very important in Polynesian culture, so tattooing became a status symbol. Different designs identified special tribal members such as chiefs or great warriors. Maori chiefs were so closely identified by their special *moko* that they could use a drawing of their tattoo as their signature on legal documents. A Samoan man could not be made a chief without tattoos. Even today, Samoan men may not be allowed to enter the house of a chief without a tattoo. Samoan women would not be given the honor of serving a ceremonial drink called kava unless their hands were tattooed.

The traditional process of getting a tattoo in many Polynesian cultures took a long time and was quite painful. Needles made from sharpened animal bones or teeth and bamboo were gathered together in a comblike instrument. After the needles were dipped in ink (which was generally made of sugar cane or nut juice mixed with soot), they were tapped into a person's stretched skin repeatedly for each mark.

All of this was accomplished without anesthetic. Some large, complex designs, such as the Samoan *pe'a*, could take weeks, to finish. Afterward, stinging salt water was typically washed over the tattooed skin to try to keep it clean. That is why having a tattoo was also a sign of strength and bravery in many cultures.

Other reasons that the members of Polynesian cultures got tattoos included showing loyalty to a chief, recording family ties, and demonstrating grief when a loved one died. Tattoos might also act as a picture journal of tribe members' travels and the important events in their lives.

Corset Piercings and Subdermal Implantation

An extreme form of body piercing is corset piercing. The spine or side of the torso is pierced with a series of loops in two vertical lines, through which a ribbon or cord can be laced and tied, like an old-fashioned corset. The lace can only be kept in for short periods of time. Prolonged lacing will put too much pressure on the piercings, which can lead to scarring and infection. The rings or bars should be removed as well. A corset piercing should only be performed by an experienced piercer.

Another extreme form of body modification is subdermal implantation. A silicone or Teflon object is inserted under the skin through an incision, and the shape of the object shows through on the surface. More than fifty thousand people have undergone this procedure worldwide. The medical community is concerned about this practice, as it is surgical in nature and done by piercers who may lack medical training.

Modern Samoans still consider tattooing an important cultural rite. In fact, men get the *pe'a* and women the less complicated *malu* in the same way, with the same tools, as their ancestors. In other cultures, such as the Mentawai of Indonesia, the once important practice of body art is declining. Even as some cultures move away from tattooing, their traditions are likely to live on in their designs, which are very popular with tattoo wearers everywhere.

Social and Other Groups

Couples, parents and their children, siblings, and friends may get matching tattoos as a way of bonding, or bringing them closer together. For instance, some couples have matching tattoos that proclaim their love for each other, such as having each other's names tattooed on their arms. But bonding through body art is not just for these types of relationships.

Various subcultures, meaning smaller groups within a larger culture, have made tattooing an important part of their lives. Among these groups are college fraternities and sororities, motorcycle clubs, gangs, prisoners, and social clubs or brotherhoods such as the Masons.

Fraternities and Sororities

Fraternities and sororities are social organizations that people join when they are in college. "Fraternal" means "brotherly" and "sorority" is from the Latin word *soros*, which means "sister." Members of fraternities and sororities think of themselves as brothers or sisters, respectively. This close relationship is meant to last for life, and tattoos are supposed to be a permanent reminder of that bond.

Most of these organizations use Greek letters to identify themselves. These letters make popular tattoo designs for fraternity brothers and sorority sisters. Members may also get a brand, which is a design that has been created specially for

Scottish soldiers Captain Lawrence Kerr and Major Jock Dunn got matching dragon tattoos when they were serving together in Hong Kong. The men were also childhood friends and classmates.

their organization. Instead of being applied using a needle and ink, brands are burned into a person's skin.

Bikers

Tattoos have been popular with bikers—groups of people who ride motorcycles and are enthusiastic about everything connected with these vehicles—for quite a while. In fact, bikers were among the first groups in the United States to

A woman sports a tattoo that shows her pride in being a female biker. The pink ribbon on the chassis honors friends of hers who have been diagnosed with breast cancer.

get inked, long before body art was a trend or popular in the country.

Motorcycle groups started forming in the United States after World War II. At that time only sailors and soldiers had body art. Sociologists, who study the lives of people from various cultures, believe that bikers started getting tattoos mainly because very few other people had them. They wanted a way to show their bond over motorcycles and demonstrate that they were different from the rest of society.

Tattoos are still quite popular with bikers. Common designs include skulls, wings, flames, and the logo for the type of motorcycle a group rides.

Gangs

Like bikers, gangs are another subculture with members who set themselves apart from mainstream society and are known for wearing tattoos. Along with flashing hand signs and wearing certain colors, getting a tattoo is a way that gang members identify with each other and members of other gangs.

As with fraternities, gangs may have special letters, characters, or symbols that represent their group inked onto their skin. These tattoos often tell a more complex story about the wearer than simply what gang a person belongs to. Designs might also show what rank someone holds within the gang.

While not forbidden, tattoos are discouraged in Japanese culture because of their association with gang activity. Members of the Yakuza, known as the Japanese mafia, ink large portions of their bodies with designs that are meant to show strength and an unwillingness to obey the rules of society. Restaurants and other public places in Japan have turned away anybody with a tattoo, just in case he is a member of the Yakuza.

Prisoners

In ancient Rome, some people were forced to get tattooed so that they could be identified as either slaves or prisoners.

Today, many prisoners in North America get tattoos willingly. The reason tattoos are popular in prison may be because body art is one of the only ways prisoners can express themselves in their very controlled environment. Also, gangs often form in prisons. Just as with gang members in the outside world, prisoners want a visible sign that they will be permanently loyal to their gang.

For the most part, prisoners do not have access to professional tattooing equipment. Therefore, they have to make due with what they have. Tattooing needles may be made from any piece of metal that can be found, such as a paper clip. Real ink from a ballpoint pen might be used or, like primitive tribes and cultures, prisoners might create ink by mixing the ashes from burned material with water or another fluid.

Prison tattoo designs typically feature symbols of violence and drug use. For instance, the number "13" stands for "M"—the thirteenth letter in the alphabet—which is a symbol for marijuana. Teardrops may represent either that the prisoner has lost someone close to him or has committed a murder. Chains, hourglasses, and bars signify the wearer's time in jail.

The risk of getting an infection or disease from a prison tattoo is quite high. In an effort to avoid infection and diseases such as HIV/AIDS and hepatitis among inmates, a handful of Canadian prisons have set up tattoo shops behind bars. Prisoners are trained to use sterilized, professional equipment and are taught about safe tattoo practices. Health Canada reported that 47 percent of men and 53 percent of women in Canadian prisons had tattoos.

Tattoos are common in prison populations. Some inmates, like this one in Denver, Colorado, may have had tattoos before they were arrested. More ink may be added during their time behind bars.

Think Before You Ink

Tattoos send a message to the people you meet. People may attach different meanings to those messages—some of them negative. While some people might see body art as fashion-able, hip, and adventurous, others will interpret ink as a statement against mainstream society. Others tend to think that body modification is an indication that the wearer engages in risky behaviors, such as criminal activity and drug abuse.

Put simply, having a tattoo or piercing might get a person "in" with some crowds, but keep them on the fringes of oth-ers. Anybody who thinks about getting some form of body modification should seriously consider the social implications beforehand.

CHAPTER 3

Military and Other Service

Members of a country's armed forces, the men and women who protect the public, are understandably very proud of their work. One way many members of these groups have chosen to show their pride is by getting a tattoo connected in some way to their job. Servicemen, servicewomen, and emergency personnel operate like a subculture, brought together by their work. Tattoos also help bond the people who have made a career out of these types of jobs.

Popular tattoos for military personnel include flags of their particular nation, other symbols of their country (such as the American bald eagle), the insignia or logo for their branch of service, a symbol of their squad or division, or the name of a fellow soldier who has died in battle.

History of the Tattooed Warrior

Soldiers and sailors getting tattooed is nothing new. There is written evidence that the practice goes back at least to the time of the Roman Empire, under the emperor Hadrian (117–138 CE). Unlike modern-day military personnel, however, these ancient warriors did not have a choice of designs or whether they wanted a tattoo or not. Soldiers of the Roman Legion had their hands tattooed—no one is sure what the legion mark looked like—after they had passed a fitness test. Historians think that permanently marking soldiers in this way may have been done to discourage troops from deserting, which means leaving military service without permission.

The process of getting a tattoo in ancient Rome began with coating the area to be marked with leek juice to clean the skin. Sharp tools were used to prick the skin in the shape of whatever design was used. Ink, made from mixing pine bark, bronze powder, metal sulfate, and a little more leek juice, was then rubbed over the wound. The color of the ink was then permanently embedded in the skin.

Throughout history, there have been other reasons why fighters have gotten tattoos. Warriors in some native tribes believed that certain tattooed images would act as a talisman, a mark with magical powers that would keep them safe in battle. Other groups got colorful and widespread tattoos mainly so that they would look fierce and frighten their enemies. Before going off to battle, some men got tattoos so that, if they died, they would get a proper religious burial or otherwise be allowed to cross into the spirit world.

Tattoos as Camouflage

The tattooing Web site The Vanishing Tattoo reports that eighteenth-century warriors in Hawaii and on an island chain known as the Marquesas tattooed their skin from head to toe but only on one side of their body. Apparently the heavily inked sides of their bodies helped the warriors blend in with leaves and plants in the Polynesian jungle. By showing only their inked side in battle, they were able to use their tattoos as camouflage, keeping them hidden from the enemy. The non-tattooed half of their body seems to have been their "civilian side."

U.S. Armed Forces

Members of the U.S. military keep the entire country safe, so they work for the federal government. Guidelines concerning the appearance of American servicemen and servicewomen, however, are largely ordered by each branch of the armed forces. The U.S. Army, Navy, Marines, and Coast Guard each have their own specific dress code, which includes restrictions on body modifications, including tattooing.

The Army

Until recently, the U.S. Army permitted tattoos as long as a dress uniform could cover them. Recently, however, the Pentagon announced that it is changing its rules. Reacting to a changing youth culture and record-low recruiting totals, recruiters have begun to accept applicants with some neck and hand tattoos. An article in the *Los Angeles Times* offered the following excerpt from guidelines given recruiters by the Pentagon: "All tattoos that are on the neck that are not vulgar, profane, indecent, racist, or extremist are authorized as long as it does not extremely degrade military appearance."

This soldier's tattoo—the word *Loyalty*—meets army criteria. It is not offensive or sexist, and it can be covered by the uniform's shirt sleeve, if necessary.

The policy also forbids sexist tattoos, such as "those that advocate a philosophy that degrades or demeans a person based on gender." While more liberal that past policies, the army's stand on body modification is still far from "anything goes."

The Navy

In 1796, Captain James Cook sailed to the Polynesian island of Tahiti. There he saw natives whose bodies were covered with inked symbols and designs. Upon his return to England, Cook introduced *tatu* (which morphed into the word "tattoo") to the Western Hemisphere through his writings on the

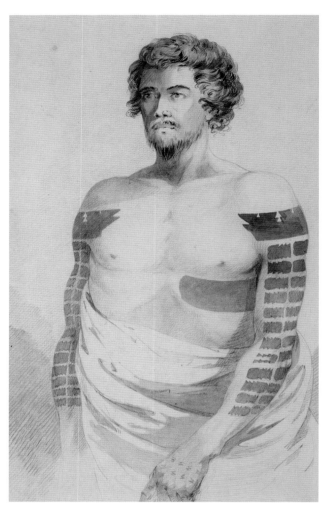

Native tattoos on the sailor's arms are clearly visible in this portrait by John Webber of a seaman on one of Captain James Cook's Polynesian voyages.

expedition. Additionally, some of the sailors on Cook's ship actually got tattooed themselves. Thus began a long tradition of seamen getting tattoos. Modern-day tattooing in the military is still most closely associated with the navy.

The rules on body modification that the U.S. Navy follows were last reviewed in 2006. Tattoos are judged by content, location, and size. Navy policy states that, as with other branches of the military, tattoos that are obscene or offensive are not permitted. Art cannot be on parts of the body not covered by clothing, especially a sailor's head, face, or neck. Tattoos also should not show through the white dress uniforms they wear while on duty. As far as size, any one tattoo cannot be larger than the wearer's hand.

Sailors or recruits with tattoos that do not meet navy requirements have the option of having their body art removed.

If they refuse to remove a tattoo or cannot have it removed for medical reasons, they will be dismissed from service.

The Air Force

According to the branch's dress and personal appearance policy, members of the U.S. Air Force are not allowed to have inappropriate artwork anywhere on their bodies. This rule applies to all ink, whether it is covered or uncovered and whether or not a member is on duty. The concern is that the air force keep its professional image. There is a limit on how many tattoos air force personnel can have as well. No more than a quarter of a member's body can be covered in body art.

In addition to the subject matter and size of tattoos, the air force has taken a special interest in the location of body art in recent years. When its policy on tattooing was reviewed in 2009, the U.S. Air Force at first decided that new recruits could not have body art on their right arms, which they use to salute. Just two weeks after that rule was made, it was changed.

The Marines

Members of the U.S. Marine Corps are allowed to have body art on parts of their bodies that are covered by their uniforms, provided they are not offensive in any way. Tattoos on the head and neck have been off limits for quite a while. As of 2007, the Corps also decided not to allow sleeve tattoos of various lengths. A full sleeve covers a person's entire arm or

A U.S. Marine in Afghanistan displays a tattoo that contains religious and military images. The words *Protect Us* are probably a reminder of the man's mission.

leg. The marines' policy on body modifications also does not allow for half-sleeve or quarter-sleeve tattoos if any part of them is visible while an enlistee is wearing his or her training uniform. A marine training uniform is made up of a short-sleeved shirt and shorts.

An exception is made for marines who are already in the service and have a sleeve tattoo. However, all existing sleeve artwork must be photographed and the photographs kept on file. Any marine who does not follow the rules regarding body art is charged with failing to follow orders, and may not be allowed to reenlist. Marines also have the option of having tattoos removed, but they have to pay for the laser removal themselves.

Coast Guard

The U.S. Coast Guard and Coast Guard Reserve have basically the same rules as the other military branches when it comes to content. There are no limits on the number of tattoos a person can have, but any body art must not be visible when wearing the standard uniform. This means that no ink can appear on the head, face, or neck. The only time a tattoo is allowed on a U.S. Coast Guard member's hands is when it is in the form of a ring. Even then, only one tattoo is allowed per hand, and that one cannot be on the person's thumb.

Canadian Forces

Members of the Canadian military, known collectively as the Canadian Forces, follow a dress code requiring that they not have tattoos that can be seen when they are in their uniform or civilian clothes. Areas of the body that are specifically discussed in the dress code are the head, neck, chest, and ears. Also, members cannot have tattoos that may be considered offensive. Under this description are images of naked bodies, quotes with profanity (swear words) or racist language, or symbols of hate groups, such as the Nazi swastika. The only piercings allowed are earrings, and those may be worn only by women service members.

Religious and Ritual Tattoos

For some, tattooing is not only about personal expression—it can also be a part of people's faith. These tattoos can be a religious symbol or even quotes from sacred texts. In some faith cultures, tattooing is discouraged, while in others it is a vital part of a person's spiritual journey.

History of Tattooing in Christianity

Tattooing was not common among early Christians. When it came to body art, they approved of the rare use of religious tattoos but strongly discouraged any other kind. For instance, a ruling by the Church of England handed down in 787 CE specifically stated that when a person receives a tattoo in God's name, "he is to be greatly praised." However, "heathen" tattooing, which was practiced by tribes of people who were not Christians, was called "superstitious." The wearer of such a mark would "derive no benefit" from this type of tattoo.

Through the Middle Ages, tattoos were permitted by the church as long as they were expressions of faith. Soldiers during the Crusades are an excellent example. In the eleventh through thirteenth centuries, Christian warriors were sent on several missions to obtain what they considered "holy land" located in the Middle East. Jerusalem was a particular point of interest because it is the place where Christians believe Jesus lived and preached. These crusaders would get tattoos that represented their journeys during what was considered righteous battle.

Modern Christians and Tattoos

Modern Christians have many different views on body modification. While most sects don't forbid tattoos, there are some groups that strongly discourage it. To back up their belief, they often refer to a Bible verse that states, "You shall not make any cuttings in your flesh for the dead, nor print any marks on you." Tattooing has also been associated with idolatry, or the worship of false gods, and is seen by some as an invitation to demon spirits.

A growing segment of Christian youths favor religious tattoos as an outward, permanent sign of their faith. They point out that Christians are not required to follow other laws set out in the Old Testament, such as restrictions on what they can and cannot eat and drink. Therefore, they believe that they shouldn't have to be against body modifications based on a Bible passage either.

A young man expresses his faith through a tattoo of a crucified Jesus. Some Christian youths associate the pain of getting a tattoo with Jesus's suffering on the cross.

Body art can strengthen the faith of young Christians in a number of ways. Some feel that the pain of getting a tattoo reminds them of the pain Jesus suffered on the cross. Religious tattoos also allow people to share their beliefs. Their body art is an icebreaker, helping them begin conversations about faith and God.

The Church of Body Modification

In September 2010, North Carolina student Ariana Iacono was suspended because her nose piercing went against her high school's dress code. Iacono argued that the piercing should be protected by the First Amendment to the U.S. Constitution, which covers freedom of religion. Iacono and her mother belonged to the Church of Body Modification.

Although it is not built around a belief in a god or gods, the Church of Body Modification meets other requirements for being legally considered a church. The organization has ordained ministers, a board of directors, and a formal statement of faith. Members believe that body modification strengthens and brings together the mind, body, and soul.

After the American Civil Liberties Union took Iacono's case to court in October 2010, a federal judge ruled that Iacono should be allowed to go back to school, at least until the next hearing of her case.

Islam

In the Muslim faith, permanent tattoos are *haram*, or forbidden. Tattoos and other body modifications are criticized because they alter the creation of Allah. A Muslim who gets a tattoo risks being cursed by the prophet Muhammad, as does the tattoo artist.

Historically, not all Muslims have followed this rule. Like the Christian crusaders, some Muslim pilgrims would tattoo themselves to commemorate their trips to Mecca, their holy land. They reasoned that, after their physical death, cremation would purify them before their journey to the afterlife. In Iraq, a particular type of tattooing was quite popular until the 1930s. Called *daqq*, which translates to "to strike or knock," this form of body art was most likely brought to the region by Bedouin and Gypsy nomads.

These days, very few Muslims are tattooed. Muslim women may decorate their hands with henna tattoos, allowable because they are not permanent. Only women of this faith have piercings, and only in their ears. This tradition relates to a story about how the women of a certain town donated their earrings to the prophet Muhammad. Men are not given the option to pierce their ears. They believe it is an affront to Allah for a man to behave as a woman and vice versa.

Judaism

Within the Jewish faith, there is room for discussion about body modification. As with certain Christians, Jews who are against tattoos point to the biblical condemnation of cutting or piercing the skin. (Those who have been tattooed against their will, as in the Holocaust, or those who are tattooed for medical reasons, such as for cancer treatments, are exempted.) Those who are in favor of body modification point to verses in the Book of Exodus that describe the ancient Hebrews as having tattoos. A growing segment of Jews are embracing tattoos as an expression of their faith.

Bindi

Perhaps the most easily recognized of all tikals is the bindi, the small red dot that many Hindi women wear on their foreheads. The bindi, and many other tikals, are worn on the forehead, between the eyes in a spot called the Ajna chakra. This is the place on the human body where Hindis believe all physical and mental energy flows.

At one time these dots were used to signify when a woman of the Hindu faith was married. Nowadays, all kinds of women wear bindis, whether they are married or not. Variations of the bindi dot have become somewhat fashionable in Western culture as well. In America, a bindi is worn just for adornment. People who wear bindis for fashion often opt for a sticker bindi rather than applying it with paint or cosmetics. Sticker bindis are inexpensive, easy to apply and remove, and available in a variety of colors, shapes, and styles. Some have crystals, sequins, and tiny beads.

Hinduism

While permanent tattooing is not typical among Hindus, there are colorful body markings associated with this religion. Tikals are marks of various shapes and colors that Hindu men and women generally wear on their face to show their devotion. They are also supposed to keep the wearer healthy and protect him or her from evil spirits and bad luck. Clay, mud, ashes, or spices are made into a paste, which is used to draw temporary symbols on the wearer's skin. Symbols are usually lines or circles, but other shapes are also used.

A Hindu holy man in Nepal checks the application of tinted mud to his face in a hand mirror. Such markings are a sign of devotion.

Piercing is also part of several Hindu ceremonies. The most common is the Karnavedha, the piercing of a child's ears. It is one of the sixteen *samskara*, or sacraments, of the Hindu faith. Typically, children of either gender have their ears pierced in their third or fifth year on a holy date determined by a guru. Ancient Hindus believed that Karnavedha would protect the child from both disease and evil.

Today, all Hindu communities perform this ceremony on their children, although it is less important in some than it once was. The child's right ear is pierced first, followed by the left, and scripture verses are spoken into each ear. A wire is placed in the hole to keep it open, although boys are generally permitted to let the holes close after a while. The ceremony is followed by a celebration including a feast and almsgiving.

Less common but more extreme piercings take place in some circumstances. Veeragase is a traditional dance of celebration that sometimes includes the piercing of the mouth.

The word itself refers to the garment a soldier wears, and the dancers dress in that fashion, with various adornments, including the image of the warrior god Veerbhadra. A special type of this dance, the Puravantike, is where piercing occurs. Sometimes two dancers will pierce their lips together. Other extreme piercings, including cheek and back "cage" piercings, through which ropes are strung to pull objects, are demonstrated at festivals, such as Malaysia's Thaipusam festival, as a show of devotion.

Tribal Body Modification Rituals

Tattooing has a long history in Native American culture. In the past, tattoos were made by engraving the skin with a sharpened rock or piece of bone and then filled in with plant dyes or soot. Iroquois warriors were known to use hash marks on their thighs to show how many enemies they had killed and similar marks on their face to record battles won. Iroquois women generally confined their tattooing to therapeutic purposes, such as markings on their faces to cure or ward off head pain and toothaches.

Native Americans also received tattoos for spiritual reasons. The images of certain animals carried special traits that could be transferred to one who wore an image of the beast on his or her body. Images of wolves are particularly popular in Native American culture. The wolf is considered clever and loyal. Eagles and coyotes are other popular choices.

Yantra

In some cultures, tattoos can be used for meditation and protection. The yantra tattoo, popular in Cambodia and Thailand, is believed to protect the wearer from evil spirits and guarantee a good life. A holy person chooses for each tattoo recipient a special image from designs that have been handed down for years.

A ceremony marks the application of this very special tattoo. After receiving the yantra, five candles and five sticks of incense are lit to represent the five incarnations of the Buddha. The wearer, called a disciple, may not speak for three days and nights. To keep the protective power of the tattoo, the disciple must also make a lifelong commitment to follow other rules, such as taking one spouse only and not walking under houses (many homes in this part of the world are built on stilts). They must live an honest and humble life or the yantra will lose its power.

CHAPTER 5

Fashion

You have been presented with many thoughtful reasons why a person would choose body modification. The appearance of a tattoo or piercing is equally important. Body modifications can be seen as cosmetic enhancements, like a hairstyle or makeup. Because of its permanence, when people choose a tattoo or piercing, they should select one that they find attractive.

Tattoos as Art

Tattoos were associated with the lower class until the 1970s, when a group of new artists began embracing tattoo art. Armed with fine arts backgrounds, people such as Don Ed Hardy brought Japanese, Samoan, and Native American tattoos into vogue. They legitimized tattooing as a way to embrace diverse cultures.

Western designs had traditionally been of a single image, but these "new" designs took up larger portions of the body and were less

A model struts down an Australian runway in clothing inspired by the time-less work of tattoo artist Don Ed Hardy. Fashions with Hardy's designs are quite popular in the fashion world.

literal. A traditional tattoo of a heart or rose is easy to understand, but these complicated patterns and images were not as easy to figure out. Still, tattoos were hardly mainstream. They generally were placed where clothing could cover them.

Tattoo and Piercing Trends

In the early days of the twentieth century, a customer would choose his or her tattoo from the shop's "flash," a selection of predrawn images displayed on the walls of the shop. These images were traced onto the body and then permanently inked and filled. Today, many artists prefer that the customer help create his or her design so that it is a unique work.

In tattooing today, anything goes. Tattoo styles are borrowed regularly from other cultures. Celtic tattoos, which are a tribute to Irish and Scottish heritage, are one popular choice. Designs are generally taken from the Book of Kells, a lavishly illustrated edition of the four gospels of the Bible. Features of the art in this book include crosses, complicated knots, and detailed scrollwork.

Chinese-inspired tattoos are also common, particularly written characters and dragons. The most common characters represent values or ideals such as love, strength, and peace. Inkers recommend that before one gets a character tattoo, he or she ensures that the meaning is what the wearer intends. Because Chinese writing is not like the Western alphabet, and each stroke must be precise or the meaning is changed, verifying the translation is extremely important.

Gothic tattoos appeal to those with a dark side. Popular with goth music fans, these images reflect death and fantasy. Pentagrams are featured but are not meant to be satanic. Goths use them to represent the four elements. Fairies, flowers, vines, and bones are other pictures that may be included in a goth tattoo.

Here is a manuscript page from the Irish Book of Kells. Art copied from or similar to the work from this manuscript is popular with tattoo fashionistas.

Another trend involves sleeve tattoos, which are images that cover the arms from shoulder to wrist. They can be one unified image or many separate images linked by scrollwork or another pattern to "fill in" the sleeve. Tattoos that cover large portions of the leg are also referred to as sleeves. These tattoos must be carefully planned before beginning, and the wearer must be ready to endure several sessions to complete the work at a price that can run into the thousands.

It has been estimated that up to 25 percent of tattoos inked in the past few years are on the neck. Small symbols such as stars, flowers, and skulls are best suited for the neck. Tattoos applied to the neck are slow to heal because of the frequent movement caused by turning the head. The designs of neck tattoos may need to be reinked after the initial wounds heal.

Ask Dr. Jan, Psychologist

Q: I want to get a tattoo on the inside of my lower arm. But then somebody told me I'll never be able to get a decent job. Is that really true? Tons of people have tattoos!

A: Many companies in fact do have policies against body art and piercings. While some employees have challenged this in court, to date the companies have won in most cases. Also, employees are often required to remove piercings and cover tattoos while at work. A company's position is typically that the employee is a representative of the company and must maintain a professional and businesslike appearance.

Even the U.S. Marine Corps now restricts tattoos. Its four criteria are content, location, size, and effect of associating the Marine Corps and the Marine Corps uniform with the tattoo. If a marine has a tattoo that is not in keeping with these standards, he or she is required to have it removed at his or her own expense.

Getting a tattoo is a major decision because it can be a lifelong decision. While it's possible to have tattoos removed, the process can be costly and in some cases even more painful than getting the original tattoo.

Think about the reasons that you want to get a tattoo. And consider that there are lots of different ways to express yourself through your appearance, like your clothes and hair. Instead of getting a tattoo, you may want to consider other forms of less permanent self-expression.

Dr. Jan Hittelman is a licensed psychologist with over twenty years of experience working with teens, children, adults, and families in a variety of settings. He publishes an online question-and-answer column for teens in the Rosen Publishing Group's online resource Teen Health & Wellness.

Body Modification and Dress Codes

Some school dress codes prohibit visible body modifications. Students in schools with such policies may be forced to remove jewelry from piercings and cover their tattoo during school hours. Breaking dress code rules could lead to expulsion. Students need to weigh the importance of expressing themselves through body modification against the importance of attaining their educational goals. In cases such as this, having a tattoo quickly becomes more than an aesthetic choice.

It is important to note that school is not the end of these struggles. These types of issues follow many adults into the workplace. While there is evidence that body modifications are becoming more common and acceptable, they are a long way from American standards of business casual. In many instances, employers may ask that workers cover visible tattoos or remove jewelry while working. This is absolutely legal. Employers are permitted to impose dress codes as long as they do not discriminate based on an employee's gender, race, skin color, ethnicity, religion, or age.

Mehndi

There is a fashion alternative to permanent tattooing. Mehndi are long-lasting and intricate designs that are painted on the skin with paste made from henna leaves, which are ground into a powder and mixed with liquids such as eucalyptus oil.

Mehndi designs are plentiful and quite intricate. The effect can make a woman's hand look like it is covered with a beautiful lace glove.

The henna paste is painted on the skin with a brush or penlike bottle. The paste dries over a period of several hours and is then peeled off, leaving an auburn-colored design on the skin. The wearer must not let water touch the dye for twelve hours; the more frequently the area is washed after this period, the faster the dye will wear off.

Mehndi (also called mehendi or mehandi) has a long history of being used in places such as the Middle East, North Africa, and South Asia. Egyptian mummies have been found with henna-colored nails and hair. Hindu goddesses are often depicted with henna tattoos, and the prophet Muhammad's wife was said to have used henna on her nails.

Like a tattoo, henna is applied to any body part, although it is traditionally found on the hands, feet, and sometimes the face in ornate designs. Designs can be small symbols or elaborate patterns that cover the entire area. Mehndi is reserved for special occasions, such as weddings. While tattoos are permanent because the ink is injected deep into the skin, henna merely dyes the top layers of skin, which are naturally shed over time, making it possible for wearers to experience up to four weeks of the mehndi without committing to a permanent design.

Changing Fashions

One special consideration when getting a tattoo or piercing for fashion's sake is what's going to be considered fashionable in the future. Clothing, accessories, hairstyles, and makeup change from year to year—sometimes even more often than that. Just because getting a tattoo or piercing is currently trendy doesn't mean it will still be farther down the road. Clothing styles that are no longer popular can be replaced. Because it is extremely difficult to remove tattoos and all traces of a piercing, body modification is permanent.

Anyone thinking about getting a tattoo should also consider that a person's tastes are going to change as he or she gets older. Certain designs may not age well. A skull and crossbones may look dangerous on a teenager or someone in their twenties but would seem kind of weird on a sixty- or seventy-year-old grandparent. People should think before they ink.

GLOSSARY

adornment Something that adds beauty.

affront To disrespect or insult.

almsgiving A donation to the poor or a charity.

bindi A colorful dot worn by Hindu women as a sign of religious devotion; placed in the middle of the forehead, the bindi may also be called a third eye.

commemorate The practice of remembering someone or something through a ceremony or a physical sign of some kind.

corset A stiff undergarment worn on the torso that is laced to tighten.

crusader A Christian soldier who fought to reclaim holy land in the Middle East from the eleventh through thirteenth centuries.

embed To place something, as an object, within or under another thing.

insignia A sign that represents membership in a group or society.

legitimize To make lawful or raise up to certain standards.

mehndi The application of intricate temporary designs on the body, especially the hands and feet, with a henna paste.

memento A reminder of the past or of something or someone that has been lost.

modification A change or adjustment to something's natural form.

pigment A substance used to add color.

sleeve tattoo One large tattoo, or a series of smaller tattoos that are somehow connected, that covers the entire arm or leg.

subculture A group that is taken from, or part of, a larger culture.

subdermal Located under the skin.

talisman Something that supposedly has the power to ward off evil.

therapeutic Something that heals or cures.

tikal A mark of Hindu devotion worn on the face.

FOR MORE INFORMATION

American Academy of Micropigmentation

2709 Medical Office Place

Goldsboro, NC 27534

(800) 441-2515

Web site: http://www.micropigmentation.org

The American Academy of Micropigmentation aims to ensure and improve the quality of micropigmentation through certification and encourages continuous learning opportunities.

Association of Professional Piercers

P.O. Box 1287

Lawrence, KS 66044

(888) 888-1277

Web site: http://www.safepiercing.org

The Association of Professional Piercers is a nonprofit health and safety organization. It distributes information about body piercing to an international audience through publications, manuals, and conferences.

Christian Tattoo Association

115 West Mulberry Street

Kokomo, IN 46901

(765) 461-3081

The Christian Tattoo Association brings together Christians interested in body art by bringing a Christian voice to the tattoo industry and subculture.

Empire State Tattoo Club of America

P.O. Box 1374

Mount Vernon, NY 10050

(914) 664-9894

Professional tattoo artists and individuals with tattoos make up the membership of the Empire State Tattoo Club of America, which sponsors body art competitions and works to increase public awareness about all aspects of tattooing.

National Tattoo Association

485 Business Park Lane

Allentown, PA 18109

(215) 433-7261

Web site: http://www.nationaltattooassociation.com

The National Tattoo Association promotes tattooing as an art form while seeking to make the process of getting inked as safe and hygienic as possible.

Web Sites

Due to the changing nature of Internet links, Rosen Publishing has developed an online list of Web sites related to the subject of this book. This site is updated regularly. Please use this link to access the list:

http://www.rosenlinks.com/ttt/ba

FOR FURTHER READING

Allen, Tricia. *Tattoo Traditions of Hawaii*. Honolulu, HI: Mutual Publishing, 2006.

Currie-McGhee, Leanne K. *Tattoos and Body Piercing*. San Diego, CA: Lucent Books, 2006.

Gay, Kathlyn, and Christine Whittington. *Body Marks: Tattooing, Piercing, and Scarification*. Brookfield, CT: Twenty-first Century Books, 2002.

Gilbert, Steve. *The Tattoo History Source Book*. New York, NY: Powerhouse Books, 2004.

Green, Terisa. *Ink: The Not-Just-Skin-Deep Guide to Getting a Tattoo*. New York, NY: NAL Trade, 2006.

Hardy, Don Ed. *Ed Hardy Art for Life*. Kempen, Germany: teNeues, 2009.

Hardy, Lal. *The Mammoth Book of Tattoos*. Philadelphia, PA: Running Press, 2009.

Kiesbye, Stefan, ed. *Body Piercing and Tattoos*. Farmington Hills, MI: Greenhaven Press, 2009.

Levey, Janey. *Tattoos in Modern Society*. New York, NY: Rosen Publishing, 2008.

Levin, Judith. *Tattoos and Indigenous Peoples*. New York, NY: Rosen Publishing, 2008.

Parry, Albert. *Tattoo: Secrets of a Strange Art*. Mineola, NY: Dover Publications, 2006.

Porterfield, Jason. *Tattoos and Secret Societies*. New York, NY: Rosen Publishing, 2008.

Sawyer, Sarah. *Frequently Asked Questions About Body Piercing and Tattooing*. New York, NY: Rosen Publishing, 2009.

Silvester, Hans. *Natural Fashion: Tribal Decoration from Africa*. London, England: Thames and Hudson Publishers, 2009.

Superior Tattoo. *Tattoo Bible: Book One*. Stillwater, MN: Wolfgang Publications, 2009.

Tattoo Johnny. *Tattoo Johnny: 3,000 Tattoo Designs*. New York, NY: Sterling Innovation, 2010.

Yi, Jian. *One Million Tattoos*. New York, NY: Thunder Bay Press, 2010.

BIBLIOGRAPHY

Anti-Defamation League. "Hate on Display: A Visual Database of Extremist Symbols, Logos and Tattoos." Retrieved December 2010 (http://www.adl.org/hate_symbols/default.asp).

Breen, Tom. "NC Teen: Nose Ring More Than Fashion, It's Faith." *Associated Press*. Retrieved November 2010 (http://news.yahoo.com/s/ap/us_rel_piercing_church).

Canfora, Nichole. "About Full-Sleeve Tattoos." eHow. Retrieved November 2010 (http://www.ehow.com/about_4727453_fullsleeve-tattoos.html).

Cavanaugh, Kerry. "New Rule Compels L.A. Firefighters to Cover Up Tattoos." *Inland Valley Daily Bulletin*. Retrieved December 2010 (http://www.firerescue1.com/labor-issues/articles/406222-New-rule-compels-L-A-firefighters-to-cover-up-tattoos).

CBC News Online. "Body Art: The Story Behind Tattooing and Piercing in Canada." Retrieved November 2010 (http://www.cbc.ca/news/background/tattoo).

Clausen, Lisa. "Sacred Skins: New Zealand's Samoans Pay the Traditional—and Excruciating—Price for Links with Their Homeland." *Time International* (South Pacific Edition), August 18, 2003, p. 90.

DeMello, Margo. *Encyclopedia of Body Adornment*. Farmington Hills, MI: Greenhaven Press, 2007.

Druzin, Heath. "Tattoos Not a Badge of Honor for Iraqis."
    Stars and Stripes. Retrieved December 2010
    (http://www.stripes.com/news/tattoos-not-a-badge-of-
    honor-for-iraqis-1.93301).

eNotAlone.com. "Tattoos Used for Medical Purposes."
    Retrieved November 2010 (http://www.enotalone.com/
    article/19619.html).

Gilbert, Steve. *Tattoo History: A Source Book*. New York, NY:
    Juno Books, 2000.

Gramza, Janet. "Tattoo Artist Helps Breast Cancer Patients
    Reclaim Their Identity." *Syracuse Post-Standard*. Retrieved
    November 2010 (http://www.syracuse.com/news/index.ssf/
    2010/11/the_art_of_reconstruction.html).

Harrison, Joyce V. "Tradition of Tattoo Art in Early Native
    American Cultures." Retrieved November 2010
    (http://www.associatedcontent.com/article/5941920/
    tradition_of_tattoo_art_in_early_native.html?cat=69).

Hollett, Jennifer. "Some Believers Get Lots of Ink." The
    (Toronto) Star.com. Retrieved November 2010
    (http://www.thestar.com/Life/article/191944).

Keinlen, Alexis. "Skin Deep: Tattoos Mark the Body's Surface.
    But Their Inspiration Draws from a Deeper Source."
    Herizons, Fall 2005, pp. 24.

Lloyd, J. D., ed. *Body Piercing and Tattoos*. Farmington Hills,
    MI: Greenhaven Press, 2003.

Love to Know. "Prison Tattoos." Retrieved December 2010
    (http://tattoos.lovetoknow.com/Prison_Tattoos).

MyJewishLearning.com. "Our Bodies: Teachings and Traditions." Retrieved November 2010 (http://www.myjewishlearning.com/practices/Ethics/Our_Bodies.shtml).

Naval Media Center. "Navy Spells Out Policy on Tattoos, Body Art, Piercings." Navy.mil. Retrieved December 2010 (http://www.navy.mil/cck/NNS060421-15.pdf).

Nickles, Steven Zyan Kain. "Air Force's New Tattoo Policy for Enlistees Under Review." DigitalJournal.com. Retrieved December 2010 (http://www.digitaljournal.com/article/283627#ixzz174LQSHyY).

PBS. "The Art and Culture of Polynesian Tattoo." *Skin Stories*. Retrieved November 2010 (http://www.pbs.org/skinstories).

Reeves, Sara. "Tattoo Art in Samoa: Volunteers Come Home with a Unique Souvenir." *WorldView*, Vol. 22, No. 1, Spring 2009, pp. 38–41.

SaTucker, Abigail. "Looking at the World's Tattoos." Smithsonian.com. Retrieved November 2010 (http://www.smithsonianmag.com/arts-culture/Looking-at-the-Worlds-Tattoos.html).

Scholgol, Jeff. "Marines Tighten Restrictions on Tattoos." *Stars and Stripes*. Retrieved December 2010 (http://www.stripes.com/news/marines-tighten-restrictions-on-tattoos-1.61843).

Schwartz, Rae. "Medical Tattoos and Micropigmentation." BellaOnline. Retrieved November 2010 (http://www.bellaonline.com/articles/art9428.asp).

Sloss, Andy, and Zaynab Mirza. *The Tattoo Sourcebook*. San Diego, CA: Thunder Bay Press, 2008.

Soldiers. "Army Changes Tattoo Policy." May 2006, p. 46.

Stanley, Deb. "Note to Police Officers: Cover Your Tattoos." 7News (Denver, CO). Retrieved December 2010 (http://www.thedenverchannel.com/news/24451668/ detail.html).

Tattoo Museum. "The Vanishing Tattoo." Retrieved November 2010 (http://www.vanishingtattoo.com/tattoo_museum).

Valentine, Bill. *Gangs and Their Tattoos: Identifying Gangbangers on the Street and in Prison.* Boulder, CO: Paladin Press, 2000.

Van Geet, Stephanie. "Tattoos and the Army: A Long and Colorful Tradition." *Fort Gordon Signal.* Retrieved December 2010 (http://www.fortgordonsignal.com/news/2009-10-02/ News_Update/Tattoos_and_the_Army_a_long_and_ colorful_tradition.html).

INDEX

About the Author

Jeanne Nagle is a writer and editor based in upstate New York. Her personal experience with body modification consists of medical and temporary tattoos, as well as pierced ears. Through comprehensive research, however, she has gained deep insight into the reasons why someone might choose to get a tattoo or piercing. She also is the author of *Tattoo Artists*, also published by Rosen Publishing.

Photo Credits

Designer: Les Kanturek; Editor: Nick Croce;
Photo Researcher: Amy Feinberg